Steal their style!

In this section you'll meet the models and see all the gorgeous clothes in our fashion show! Use the outfits to inspire you when you come to design your own collection later in the book.

This girlie, ruffled skirt is toughened up by the addition of a cropped leather jacket and ankle boots, Mixing styles like this creates an edgy, modern look.

Fashion doesn't get any cuter than this pretty, pink polka dot dress! Add a bow detail to the belt and shoes and this girl is ready to party!

Classic denim

Almost everyone has a denim item in their wardrobe and this classic fabric will never go out of fashion. Whether it be jeans, shorts, skirts or shirts – the design possibilities are endless!

MEET THE MODEL:
Olivia
Likes: Playing tennis
Dislikes: Getting up early
Fashion style: On trend

MEET THE MODEL:
Tim
Likes: Walking his dog
Dislikes: Mushrooms
Fashion style: Classic

These lovely little hotpants are perfect for lazy summer days. Brighten up a casual outfit by adding bright accessories, like these neon bangles!

Jeans look great on both girls and boys. This classic look, with white t-shirt and trainers, is cool and easy to wear. A waistcoat smartens things up a little.

MEET THE MODEL:
Rachel

Likes: Changing her hair colour
Dislikes: Spicy food
Fashion style: Playful

MEET THE MODEL:
Beth

Likes: Strawberry bubble gum
Dislikes: Cats
Fashion style: Preppy

The USA is the home of denim, so pay tribute by teaming jeans with a stars and stripes vest top! Red court shoes add a touch of glamour.

Indigo-blue denim is so fashionable and flattering. These skinny jeans worn with a funky fitted blazer and high-top sneakers scream 'college cool'!

Party dresses

Every girl needs a gorgeous party dress! Add details such as sequins, jewels and ruffles to make your designs look extra special. Choose a colour that suits your model's skin tone.

MEET THE MODEL:
Zanna

Likes: Roller skating
Dislikes: Boring colours
Fashion style: Vintage retro

MEET THE MODEL:
Kate

Likes: Going to the theatre
Dislikes: Being late
Fashion style: Sophisticated

Zanna looks beautiful in this maxi dress. The jewelled detail at the neckline and waist adds some party sparkle and breaks up the solid purple colour.

Animal print is always fun for party wear. Try using different colours rather than the classics; leopard print looks great in pink, orange and blue, too!

MEET THE MODEL:

Ava

Likes: Salsa dancing
Dislikes: Grey winter days
Fashion style: Sunny

If a bright pop of colour doesn't get you in the party mood – nothing will! This yellow dress looks amazing against Ava's skin tone.

This stunning party dress is covered in glittering sequins which catch the light and sparkle. Midnight blue is a great alternative to the classic little black dress.

Printed fabrics

Printed fabrics add detail and interest to any outfit. From pretty floral prints to polka dots and checks, try experimenting with different colours and textures in your own fashion designs.

Make a bold fashion statement by choosing an all-over print. These silk harem pants have a vintage look.

Delicate floral designs coloured in pastel shades are pretty and feminine. The print detail draws the eye to the model's top, showing off her waist.

MEET THE MODEL:
Zach
Likes: Eating out
Dislikes: Mondays
Fashion style: Smart cool

Checked patterns are simple to draw and look really effective. Create an evening look by adding a flowing maxi skirt and leopard print chain bag.

This checked shirt looks great on Zack! To give denim a slightly worn look, use lighter shades on some areas of your model's jeans.

Beach babes

Denim really does work with anything! This loose shirt is the perfect cover-up for this teeny-weeny polka-dot bikini!

Kaftans are often made from luxurious, floaty fabrics and are great for keeping cool in the hot summer sun. This fuchsia pink printed number looks fabulous on Lucy!

Bright colours and bold prints give beachwear a summery, surfer-chic look and little shorts are a great alternative to bikini bottoms.

Why not create a range of his and hers beachwear? Ava and Zack make a good-looking pair in their matching swimwear.

It's cold outside!

There are all sorts of fashionable ways to keep warm when the weather turns cold – just look at these hot looks! Choose fabrics such as faux fur and sheepskin for that ultra cosy look and feel.

Try combining different fabrics and textures. This lightweight jersey dress looks great with the heavy sheepskin jacket. Matching boots complete the look.

This faux fur coat looks and feels luxurious. Zanna has added a funky edge with these bright, studded leggings and animal print ankle boots.

The classic raincoat will never go out of fashion. For a modern look, choose a bright colour such as red, yellow or green.

The duffle coat features a mixture of textures and is full of character. Keep it looking classic with earthy colours.

Sports/utility

Why not try designing a range of fashionable new sportswear? From gym clothes to jumpsuits and cargo pants, even the most practical clothing can be stylish – just look at our models!

Use colour to link separate garments together. The red detail on Olivia's shorts, hairband and running shoes coordinates this outfit effortlessly.

Tracksuits are popular with sports stars and celebrities alike. Try different colours and patterned fabric when you design your own.

Jumpsuits are back on the catwalk! To create this loose-fitting style, draw creases and folds in the fabric.

Even cargo pants can be glamorous when worn with strappy sandals and a leather jacket!

Smarten up

A printed playsuit can be transformed into a smarter outfit by adding tights and lace-up heels. It looks great on Pixie!

Limiting yourself to two colours is an easy way to create a smart look. Even Kate's hair matches her clothes here!

This trouser suit fits Rachel perfectly. Rolling up the jacket sleeves to reveal animal print lining keeps it fun.

This classic black suit is updated with white trim, geeky specs and trainers.

Now it's your turn! Choose one of the model templates and get designing. Start by pencilling in the shape of the clothing, then add colour. Have fun creating your own catwalk collection!

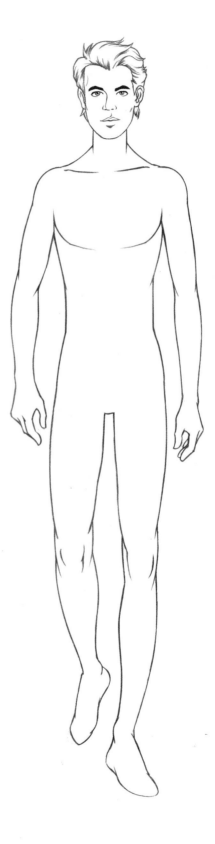

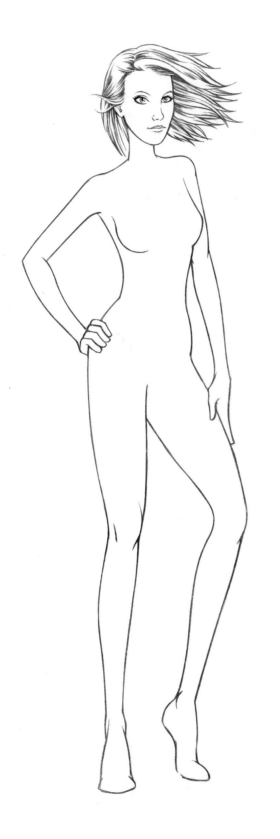
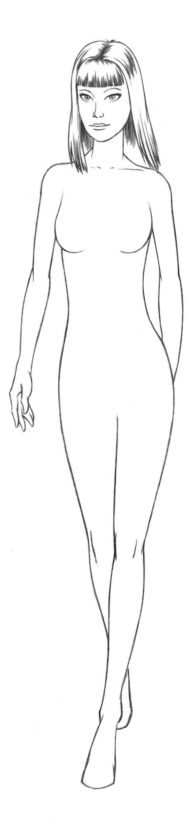

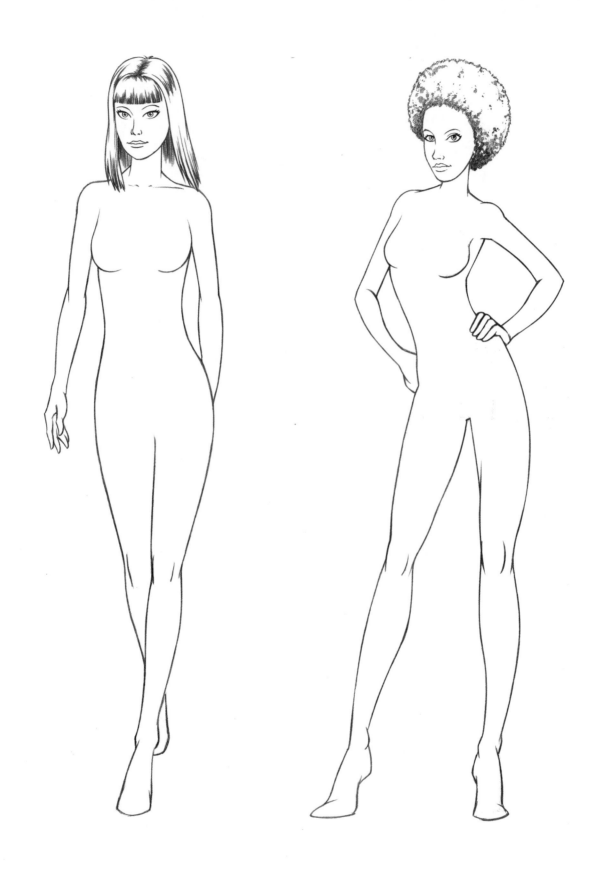

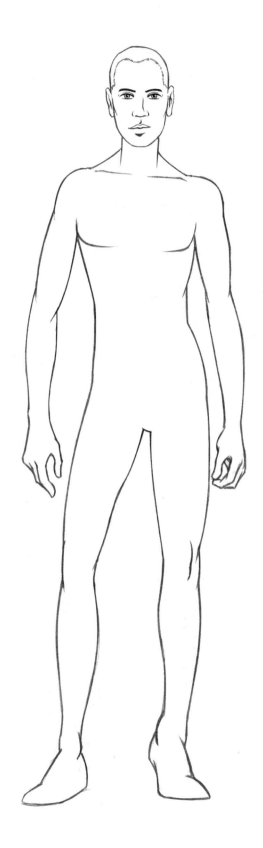
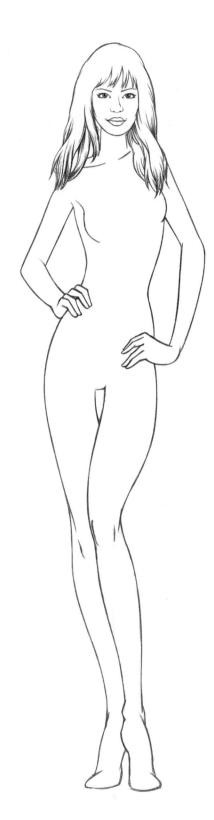

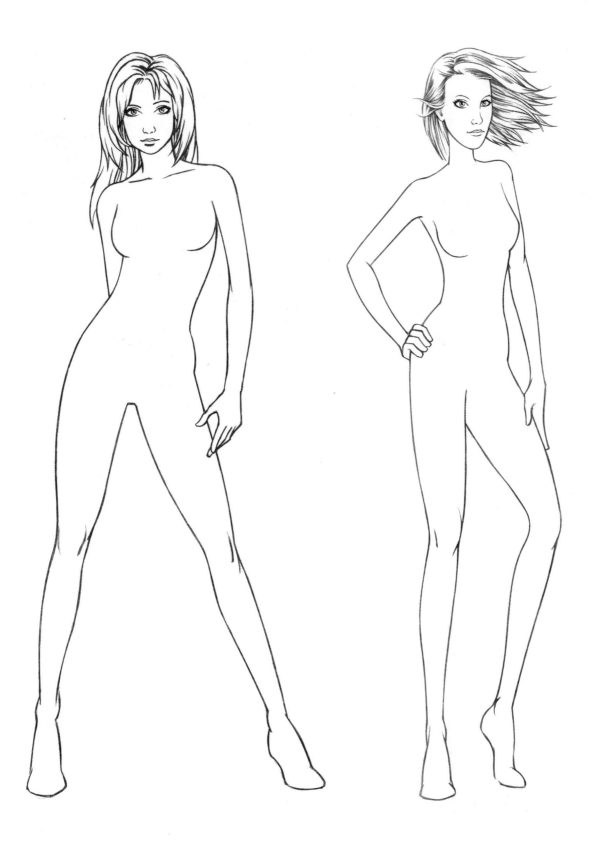

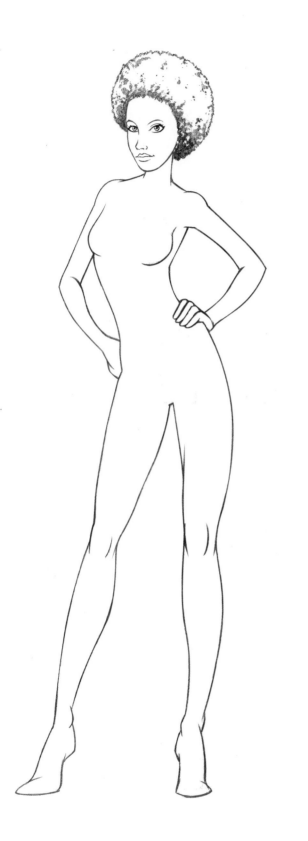
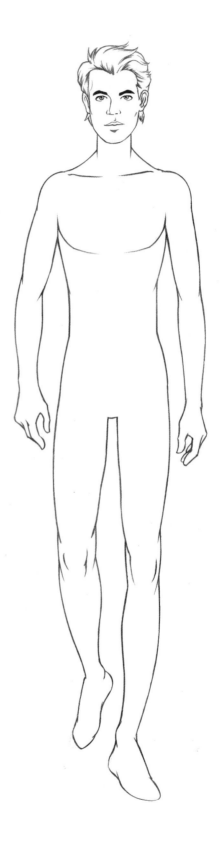

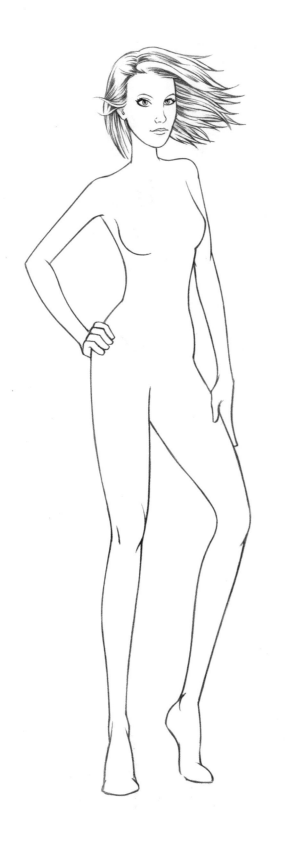
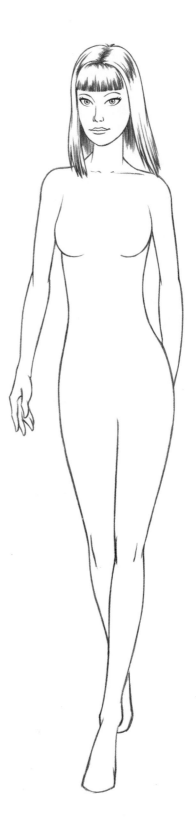

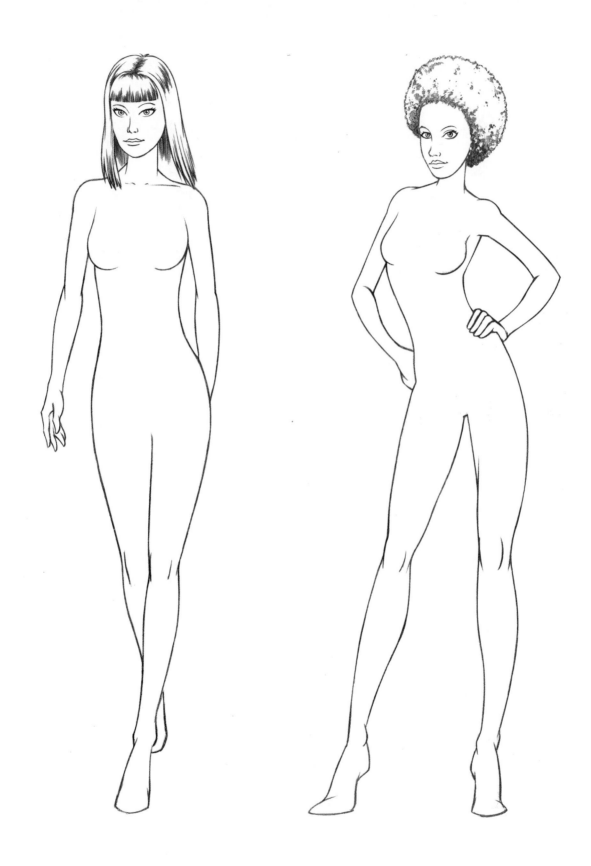

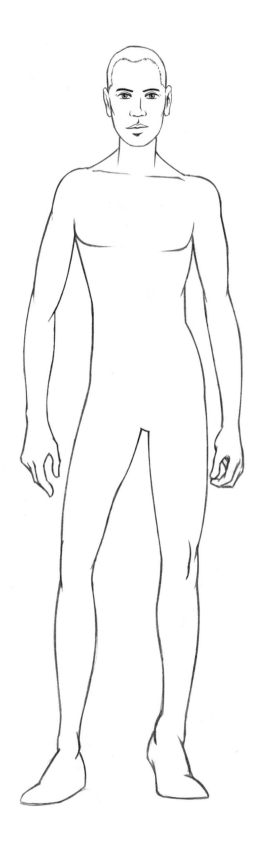
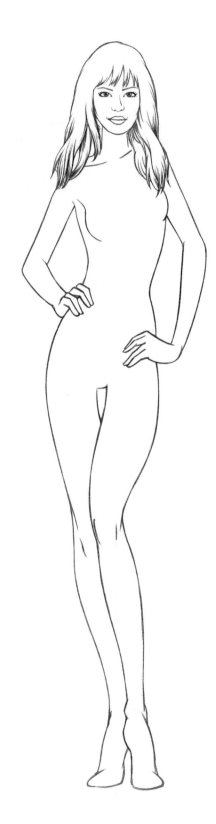

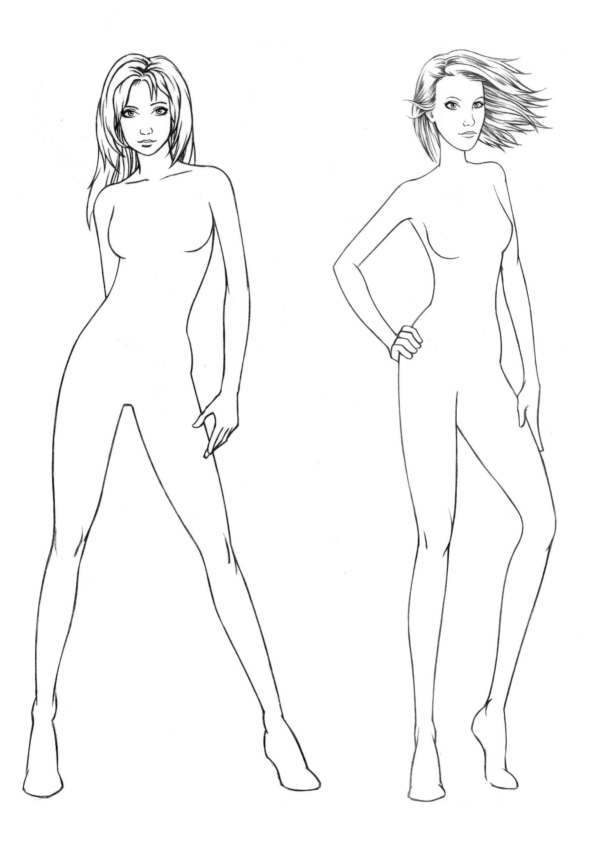

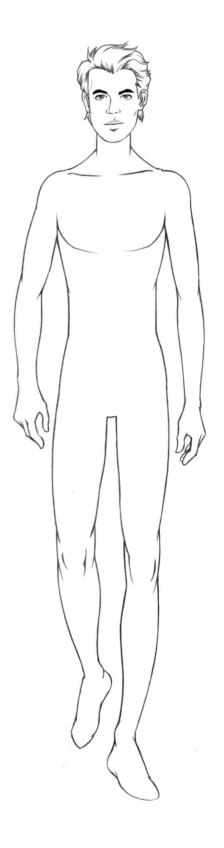

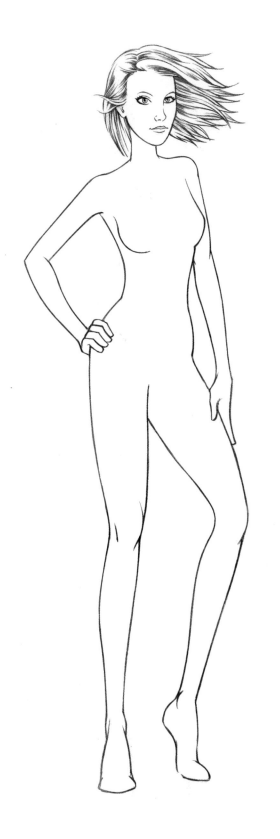
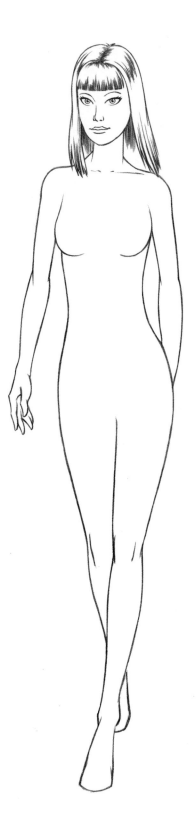

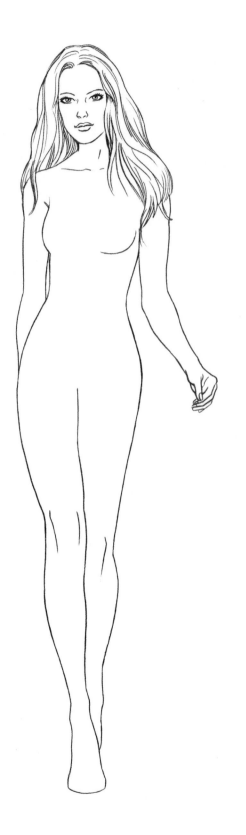
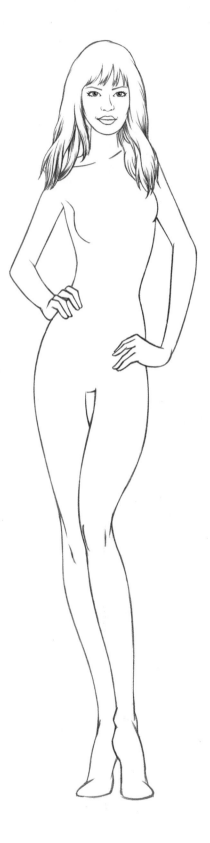

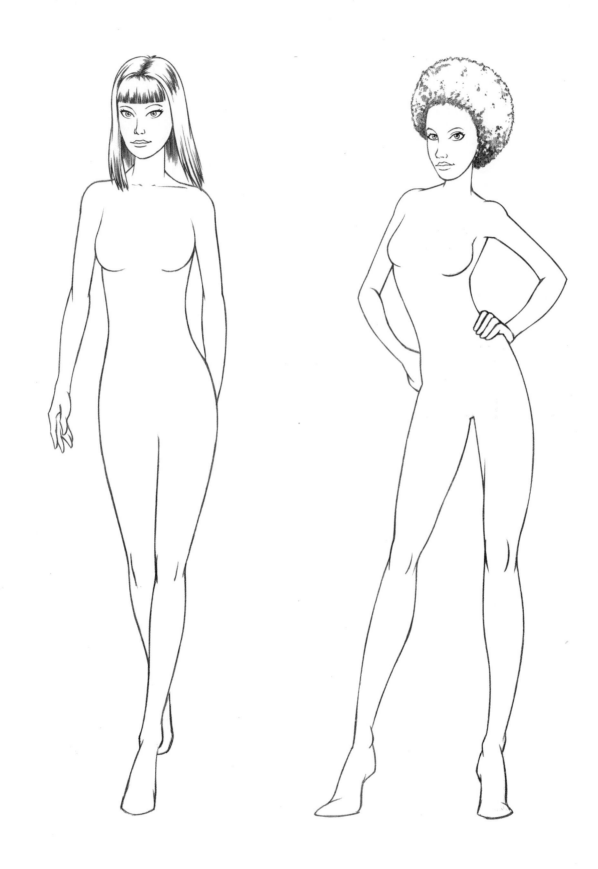

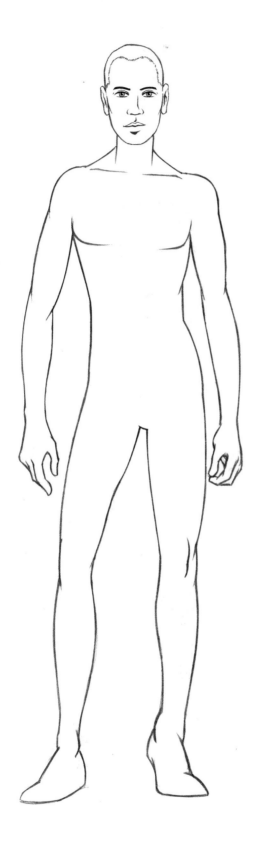
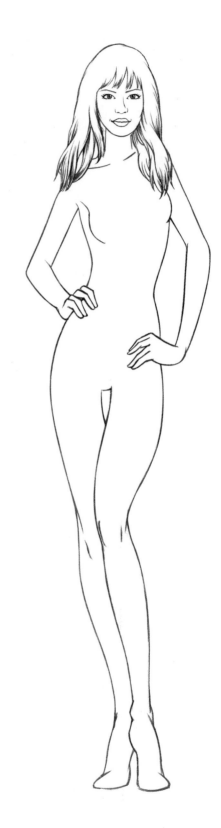

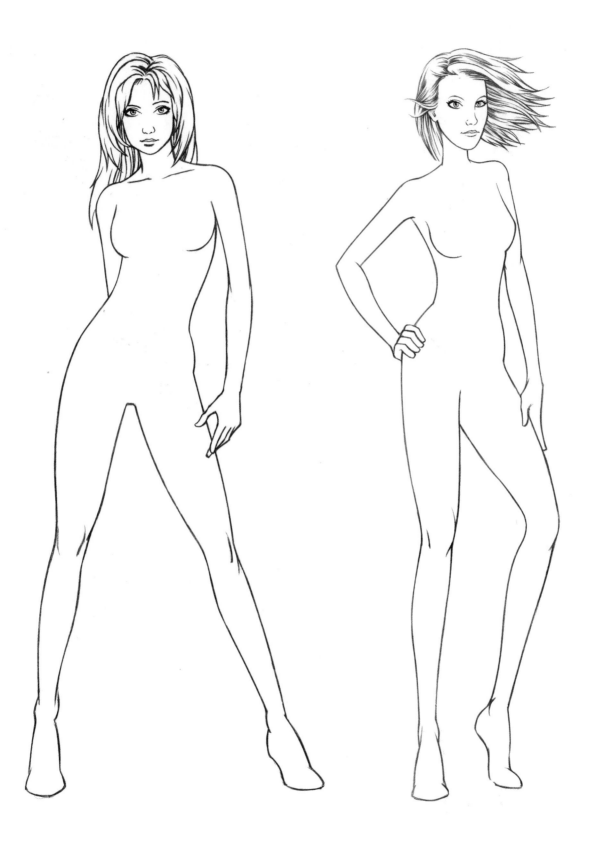

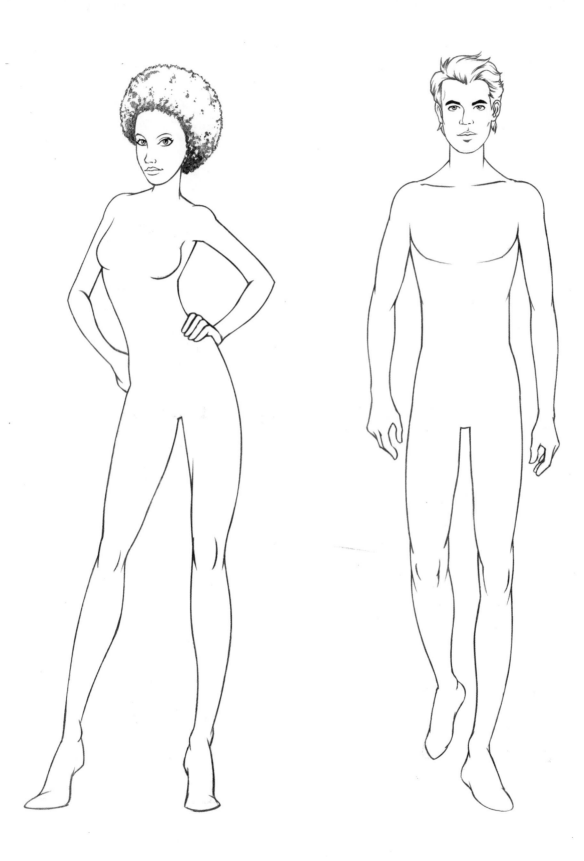

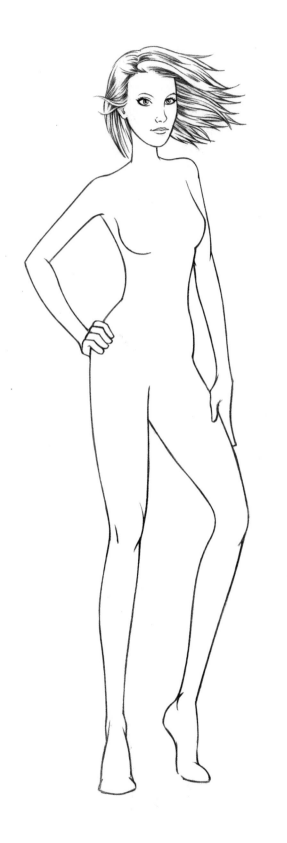
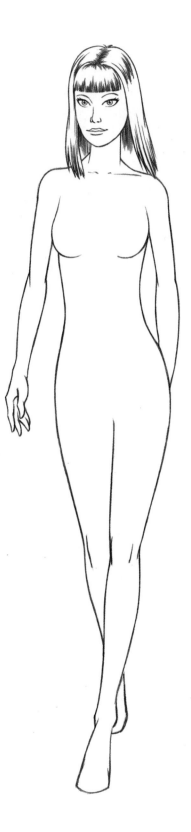

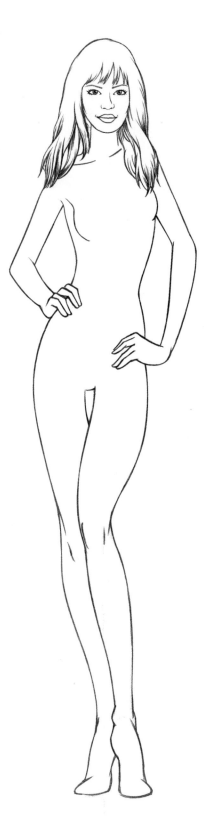

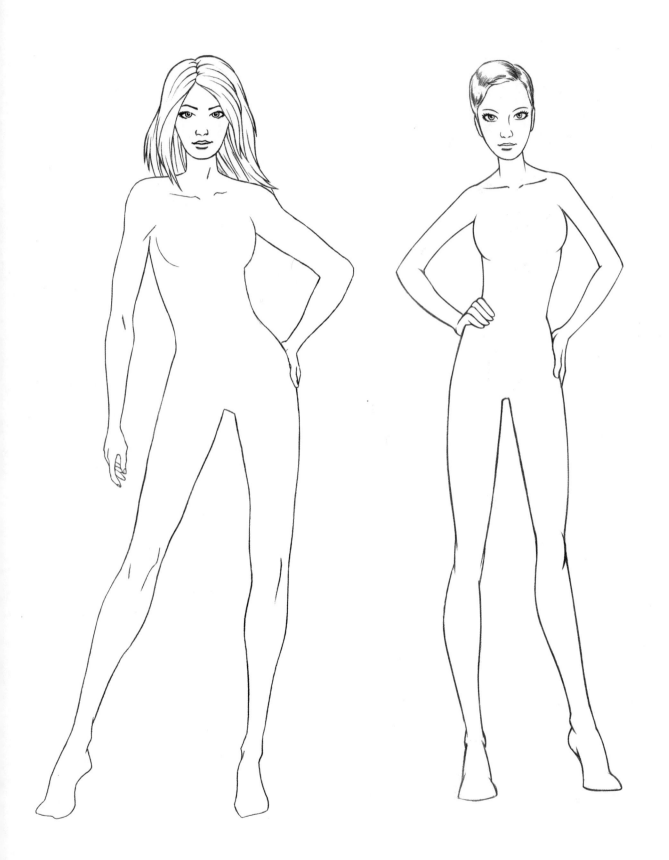

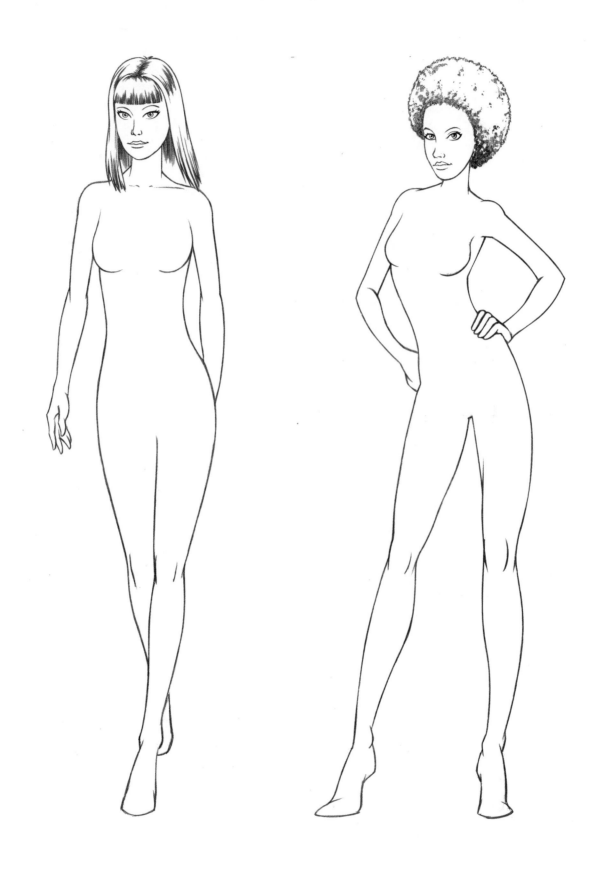

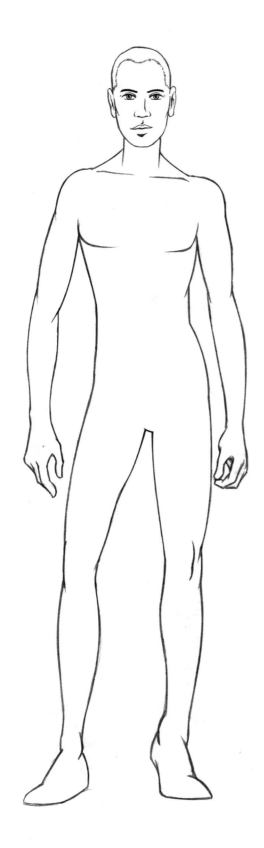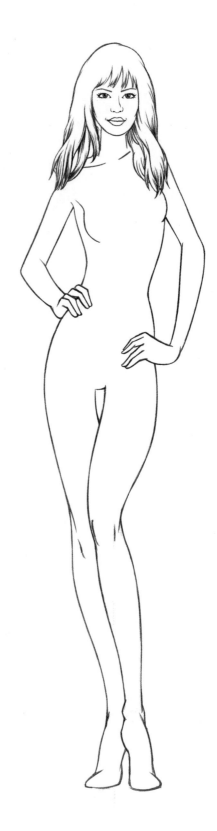

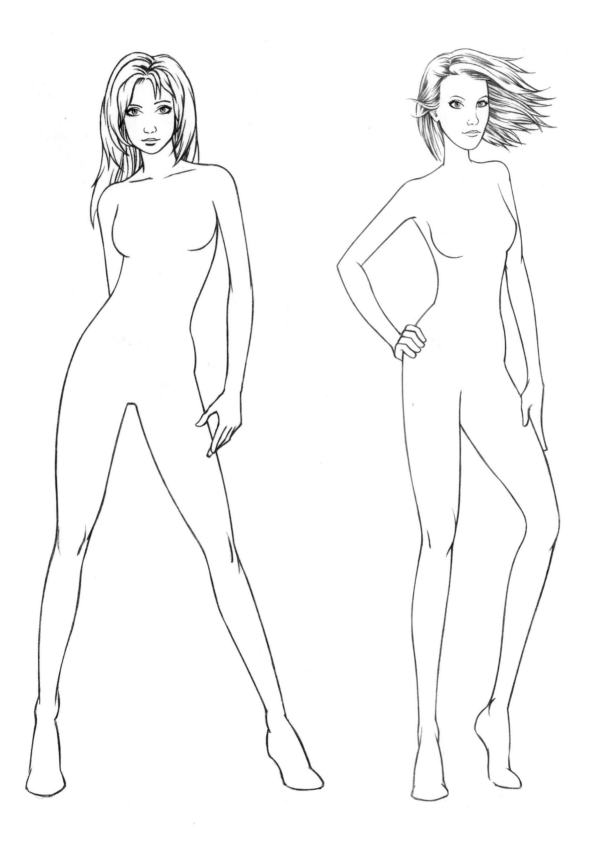

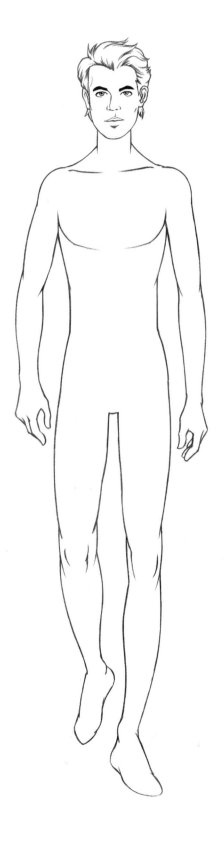

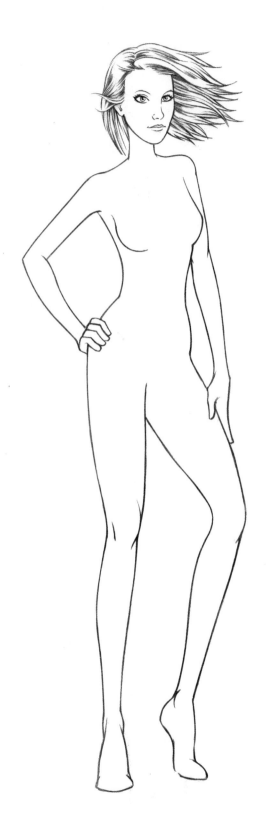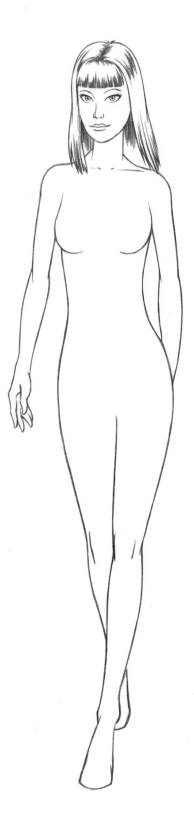

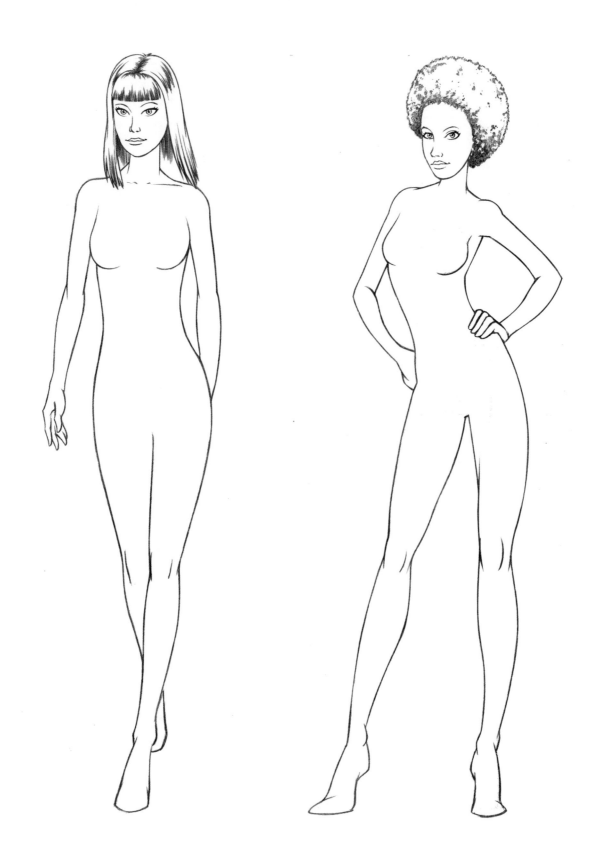

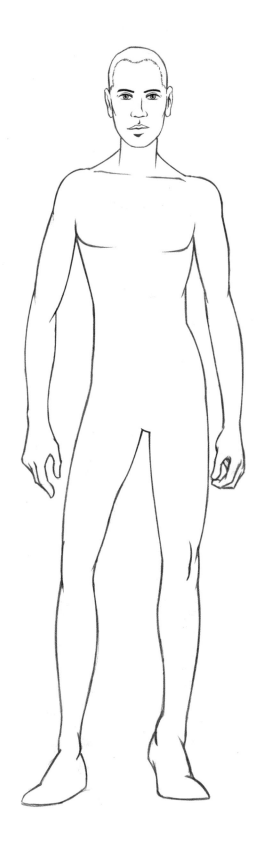
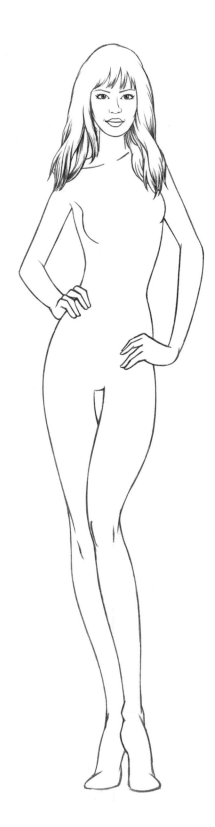

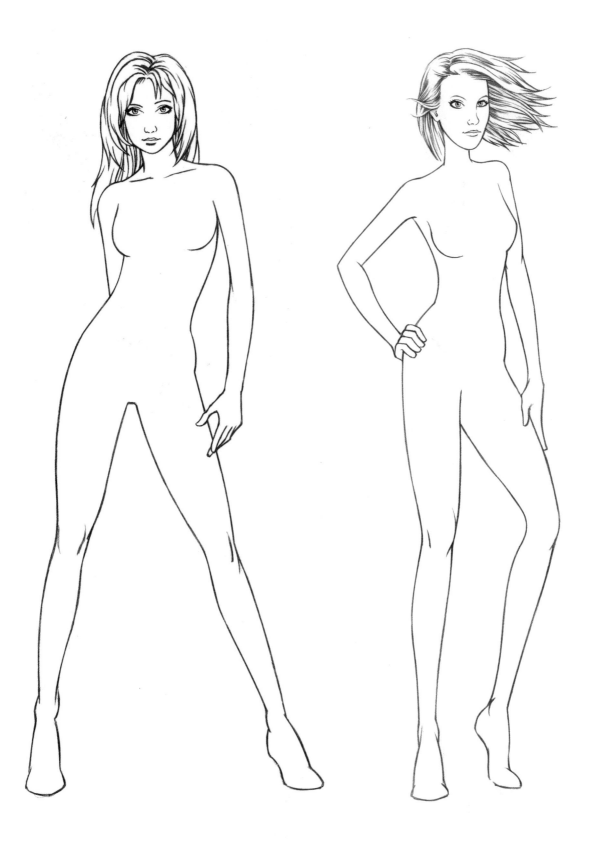

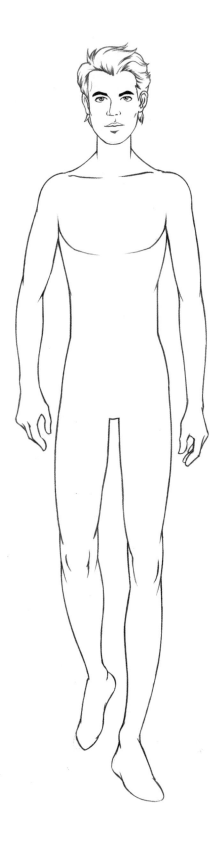

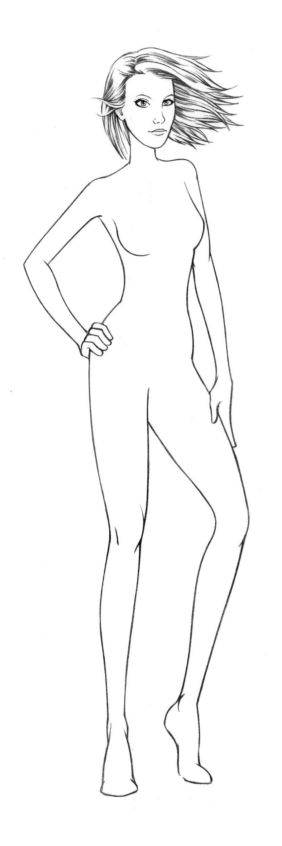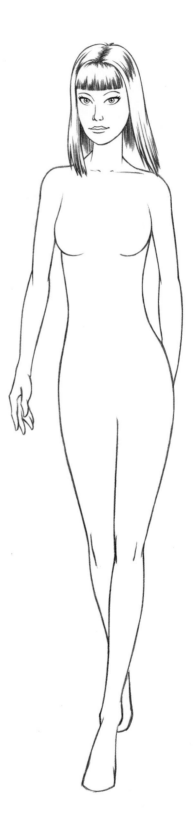

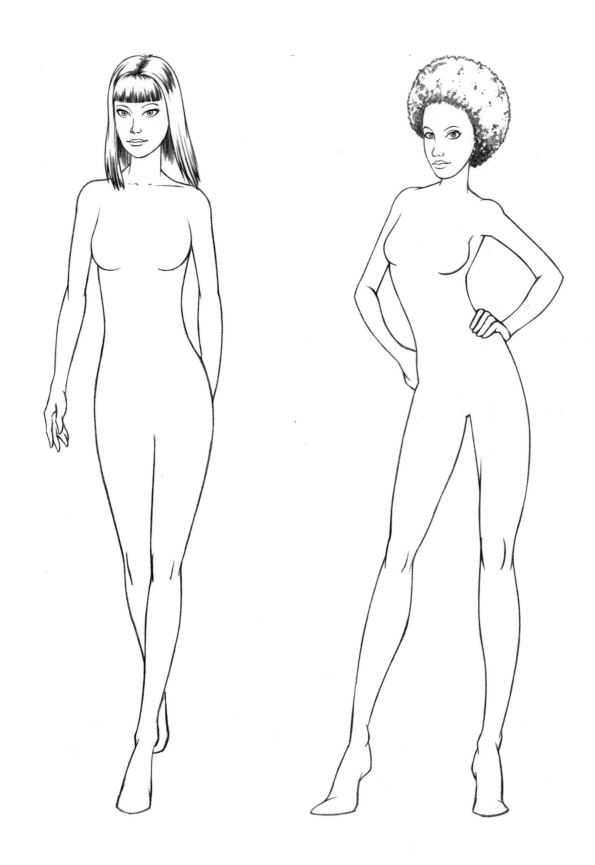

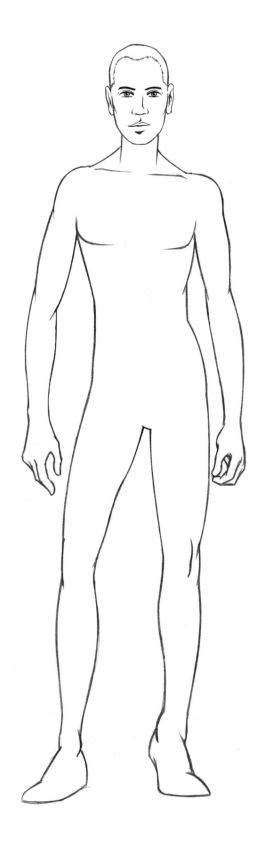
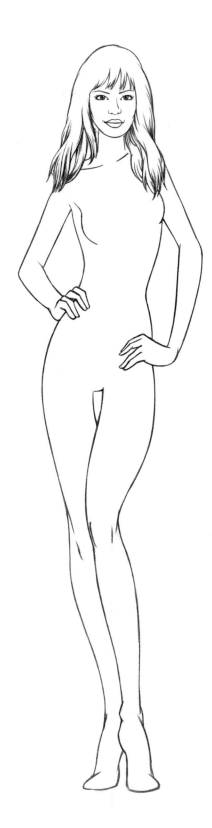

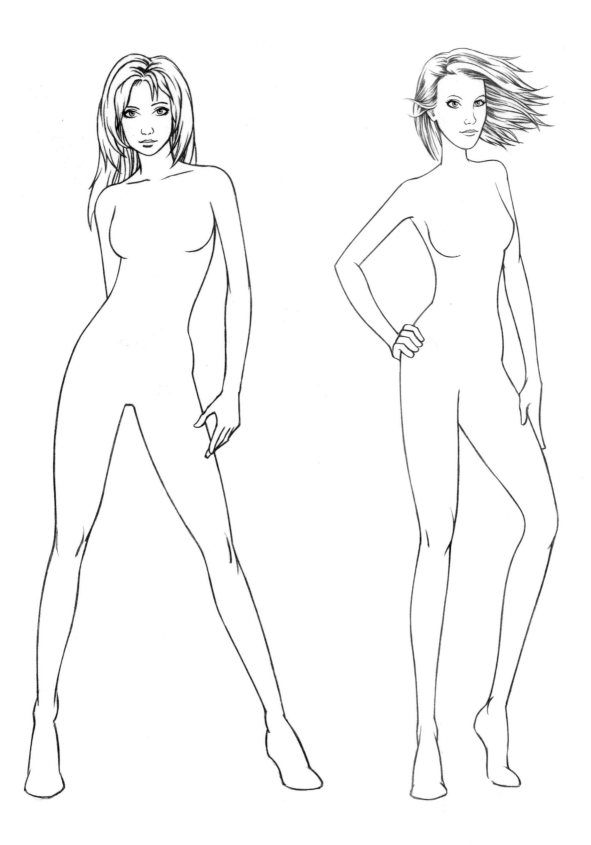

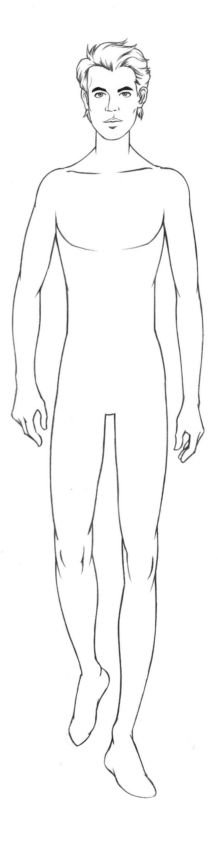

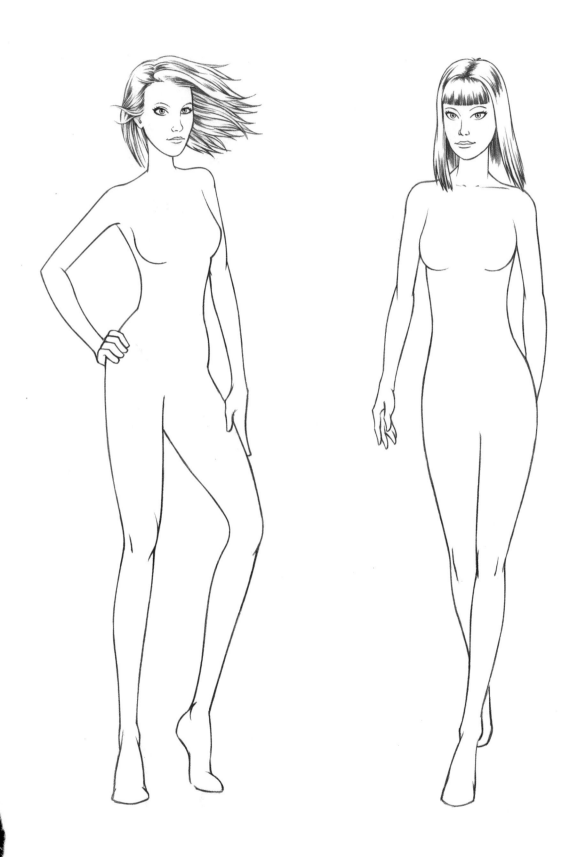